Baby Raccoons

Bobbie Kalman

Crabtree Publishing Company
www.crabtreebooks.com

It's fun to learn about Baby Animals

Created by Bobbie Kalman

Dedicated by Samantha Crabtree
To the little troublemaker Logan Keenan

Author and Editor-in-Chief
Bobbie Kalman

Editor
Kathy Middleton

Proofreader
Crystal Sikkens

Photo research
Bobbie Kalman

Design
Bobbie Kalman
Katherine Berti
Samantha Crabtree (cover)

Production coordinator
Katherine Berti

Illustrations
Barbara Bedell: pages 6, 7, 13, 14, 19,
    24 (except bottom right)
Katherine Berti: pages 9, 24 (bottom right)

Photographs
BigStockPhoto: pages 17 (bottom left), 24 (dens)
CC Lockwood: page 5
Shutterstock: cover, pages 1, 3, 4, 6, 7, 8, 9, 10, 11, 12,
    13, 14, 15 (except top left), 16, 17 (except bottom left),
    18, 19, 20, 21, 22, 23, 24 (except dens)
Other images by Digital Vision

Library and Archives Canada Cataloguing in Publication

Kalman, Bobbie, 1947-
    Baby raccoons / Bobbie Kalman.

(It's fun to learn about baby animals)
Includes index.
ISBN 978-0-7787-3963-0 (bound).--ISBN 978-0-7787-3982-1 (pbk.)

    1. Raccoon--Infancy--Juvenile literature.
I. Title. II. Series: It's fun to learn about baby animals

QL737.C26K34 2010   j599.76'32139   C2009-905192-3

Library of Congress Cataloging-in-Publication Data

Kalman, Bobbie.
  Baby raccoons / Bobbie Kalman.
      p. cm. -- (It's fun to learn about baby animals)
  Includes index.
  ISBN 978-0-7787-3982-1 (pbk. : alk. paper) -- ISBN 978-0-7787-3963-0
(reinforced library binding : alk. paper)
  1. Raccoon--Juvenile literature. 2. Raccoon--Infancy--Juvenile literature.
I. Title. II. Series.

  QL737.C26K34 2010
  599.76'32139--dc22

                                                          2009034820

Crabtree Publishing Company

www.crabtreebooks.com   1-800-387-7650

Printed in China/122009/CT20090915

Published in Canada
Crabtree Publishing
616 Welland Ave.
St. Catharines, Ontario
L2M 5V6

Published in the United States
Crabtree Publishing
350 Fifth Ave.
59th floor
New York, NY 10118

Published in the United Kingdom
Crabtree Publishing
Maritime House
Basin Road North, Hove
BN41 1WR

Published in Australia
Crabtree Publishing
386 Mt. Alexander Rd.
Ascot Vale (Melbourne)
VIC 3032

What is in this book?

What is a raccoon?

A raccoon is an animal called a **mammal**. Mammals have hair or fur on their bodies. Raccoons have fur on their bodies. Mammals are **born**. They come out of their mothers' bodies. Raccoons are born.

Raccoons have fur coats. They are mammals.

Mammal mothers feed their babies milk. The milk is made in the bodies of the mothers. Drinking mother's milk is called **nursing**. These four baby raccoons are nursing. Baby raccoons are called **kits**.

Raccoon relatives

Raccoons belong to a small family of mammals. Other mammals in this family are ringtails, kinkajous, and coatis. Scientists are not sure if red pandas are raccoon relatives or not. Giant pandas are not. They are more like bears.

red panda

Red pandas look a lot like raccoons, but are they part of the raccoon family? Red pandas live in Asia.

Coatis are great climbers.
They sleep in trees. Coatis live
in South and Central America.

The coati pokes its long nose into plants to find food.

Ringtails, or ring-tailed cats, live in the southwestern United States and in Mexico.

Kinkajous live in the forests of Central and South America.

A raccoon's body

A raccoon has four legs. It walks flat on its feet. Raccoons have pointed **snouts** and bushy tails with rings. The black patches around the eyes of a raccoon look like a mask.

The nose and mouth are on the snout.

A raccoon's tail has black rings.

Raccoons are **warm-blooded**. Warm-blooded animals keep their bodies warm from the inside, even in cold weather. The thick fur coats of raccoons also keep them warm.

What are vertebrates?

Raccoons are **vertebrates**. Vertebrates are animals with **backbones**. Raccoons have many other bones inside their bodies, too. All the bones make up a **skeleton**. The skeleton below is a raccoon skeleton.

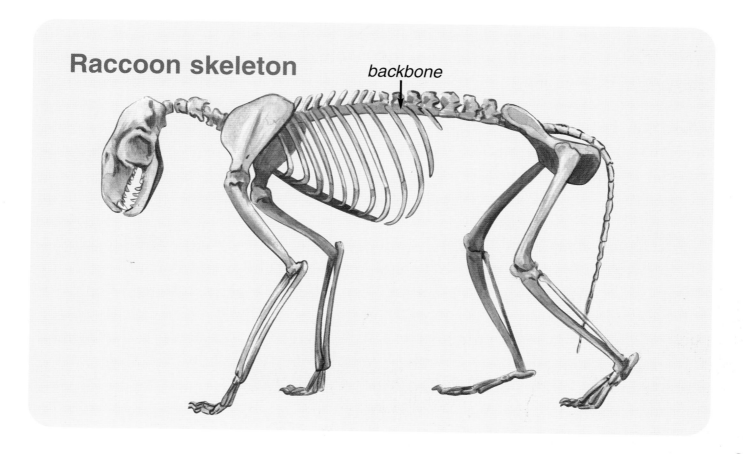

Raccoon skeleton

backbone

Raccoon senses

We have five **senses**, which are sight, hearing, smell, taste, and touch. Senses give us information about the world around us. Raccoons have good senses of touch, hearing, and smell. They cannot see very far, but they can see well in the dark. They have a **tapetum lucidum** layer at the back of their eyes. The tapetum helps them see better at night.

The tapetum reflects light and makes a raccoon's eyes appear to glow in the dark.

Raccoons have long fingers and toes.
Their fingers have curved nails called **claws**.

claws

Some raccoons wet their food, but they do not really wash it. No one knows for sure why raccoons wet their food. Maybe wetting it helps them find the right parts to eat. Their paws can feel wet things better.

Raccoons use their front paws to do many things. They use them to put food into their mouths, open locks, get into garbage cans, and grab small, thin, objects, such as this potato chip.

Raccoon babies

Raccoon mothers give birth to one **litter** of babies a year. A litter is two or more babies that are born to a mother at the same time. Raccoon litters have three to four babies, but some mothers have as many as seven kits. The kits are tiny. They have only a thin layer of fur, and they cannot see or hear. As soon as they are born, the kits start nursing.

*Mother raccoons find safe **dens**, or homes, where they give birth to their babies.*

*Dens for babies are called **nursery dens**. Many nursery dens are in tree holes.*

The life cycle of a raccoon

Animals go through a set of changes called a **life cycle**. They grow, and their bodies change. Each raccoon starts its life cycle as a baby. It is born, grows into a **juvenile**, and into an adult. When a raccoon is an **adult**, it can make its own babies. The babies then start new life cycles.

A life cycle starts with each new kit.

This litter of newborn kits is in a nursery den.

This adult raccoon is two years old. It has a kit.

These kits are six weeks old.

A juvenile raccoon is a young raccoon. This juvenile is nine months old.

The Kits explore

Raccoon kits grow quickly and stop nursing at about three months. They are then ready to look for food with their mothers. They also explore the world around them.

This kit is looking for food with its mother. The mother keeps the kit close to her.

It's a long way down!

The kits learn how to climb trees. At first, their mothers help them get down. The kits are curious and often wander away. Their mother grunts loudly when there is danger nearby.

Kits explore people's back yards.

These juveniles are fishing for dinner.

Can this kit get down on its own?

Where do raccoons live?

The natural places where animals live are called **habitats**. Raccoon habitats include **forests** and **wetlands**. Forests are habitats with many trees. Raccoons find homes and food in trees. Wetlands are habitats that are under water for part of the year. Raccoons also live near people in cities and towns. They can live in places with cold or hot weather.

Raccoons live near water. They can find fish, frogs, and other animals to eat in or near water.

Raccoons do not build dens. They find holes in trees and move in.

Many raccoons live in people's yards because they have lost their natural habitats.

What do raccoons eat?

Raccoons are **omnivores**. Omnivores eat more than one kind of food. They eat other animals, such as fish, worms, frogs, mice, and birds. They also eat eggs and plant foods such as fruit and nuts. They are **opportunistic feeders**. Opportunistic feeders eat whatever foods they find. In cities, raccoons open garbage cans and look for food that people have thrown away.

A raccoon's teeth can chew most kinds of food.

Raccoons eat bird eggs, turtle eggs, and any other eggs they find.

(left) This raccoon has found bread to eat in the snow.

Raccoons adapt

Animals **adapt** to their habitats. To adapt is to change to suit a new habitat or way of life. A raccoon's body has adapted to help it hide from **predators**. Predators are animals that hunt and eat other animals. In a forest, a raccoon's colors and markings act as **camouflage**. Camouflage helps an animal blend in with its habitat.

The colors and markings of raccoons blend in with the colors and markings of trees.

Raccoons have adapted to eating many kinds of foods.
This raccoon will eat the vegetables in someone's garden.

Raccoons have adapted to cold habitats.

Raccoons have adapted to living with people and eating their foods.

Raccoon messages

Raccoons send messages to other raccoons to share information with them. They use sounds and **body language** to **communicate**, or let others know what they want. Body language is using body movements to send messages or show feelings.

*Raccoon kits hiss, snort, and **churr**. Churring sounds like a cat purring. It means the kits are happy. Baby raccoons also hug and pretend to fight with one another.*

This raccoon bares its teeth and keeps its head low to scare away predators. It also makes growling and hissing sounds.

People and raccoons

Many people think of raccoons as pests. When some raccoons move into people's homes, they are caught in cages and taken to nearby forests. Sometimes, their babies are left behind and cannot look after themselves.

There are many wildlife centers that help baby animals. Find one in your area and ask how you can help.

Words to Know and Index

bodies
pages 4, 5,
8–9, 13, 20

camouflage
page 20

dens
pages 12, 17

eyes
pages 8, 10

food
pages 7, 11, 14,
16, 17, 18–19, 21

life cycle
page 13

messages
page 22

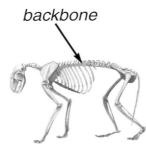
red pandas
page 6

backbone

skeleton
page 9